PICTURE LIBRARY

BMX BIKES

PICTURE LIBRARY
BMX BIKES

Norman Barrett

Franklin Watts

London   New York   Sydney   Toronto

© 1987 Franklin Watts Ltd

First published in Great Britain
    1987 by
Franklin Watts Ltd
12a Golden Square
London W1R 4BA

First published in the USA by
Franklin Watts Inc
387 Park Avenue South
New York
N.Y. 11016

First published in Australia by
Franklin Watts
14 Mars Road
Lane Cove
2066 NSW

U.S. ISBN: 0-531-15138-7 (pbk)
US ISBN: 0-531-10272-6
Library of Congress Catalog Card
Number 86-50638

Printed in Singapore

Safety note
"BMX" bicycle riding can be
dangerous. Always ride with a
helmet and other recommended
safety equipment.

Designed by
Barrett & Willard

Photographs by
Action Plus

Illustration by
Rhoda & Robert Burns

Technical Consultant
Richard Francis

Contents

Introduction

With a BMX bike, you can take part in races and other competitions. Anyone who has a BMX bike is a BMXer, whether he or she competes for big prizes or just uses it to ride to school or to run errands.

Races are staged on special tracks. The other form of competition is freestyle, which involves tricks and displays.

△ A line of BMXers stand on their pedals as they charge down the starting ramp, fighting for the lead.

6

One of the most noticeable things about a BMX bike is its tires. These are tough, with a dirt-gripping tread, and smaller than those of most other road and racing bikes.

Other features of BMX bikes include their high, braced handlebars, low triangular frame and single gear. The gearing may be altered by using another chainring.

△ A spectacular display of mid-air trickery. In freestyle competition, points are awarded by a panel of judges.

The BMX bike

Mag wheel
for freestyle

Spoked wheel
for racing

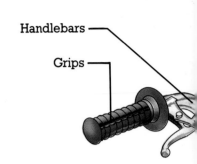

Handlebars

Grips

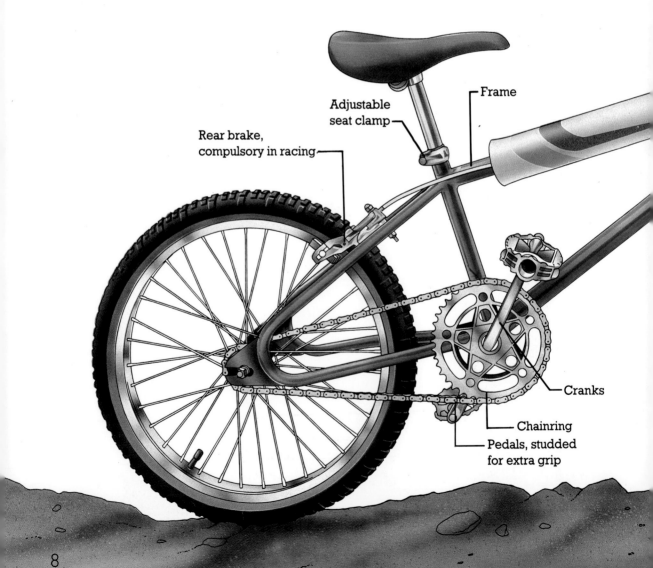

Adjustable
seat clamp

Frame

Rear brake,
compulsory in racing

Cranks

Chainring

Pedals, studded
for extra grip

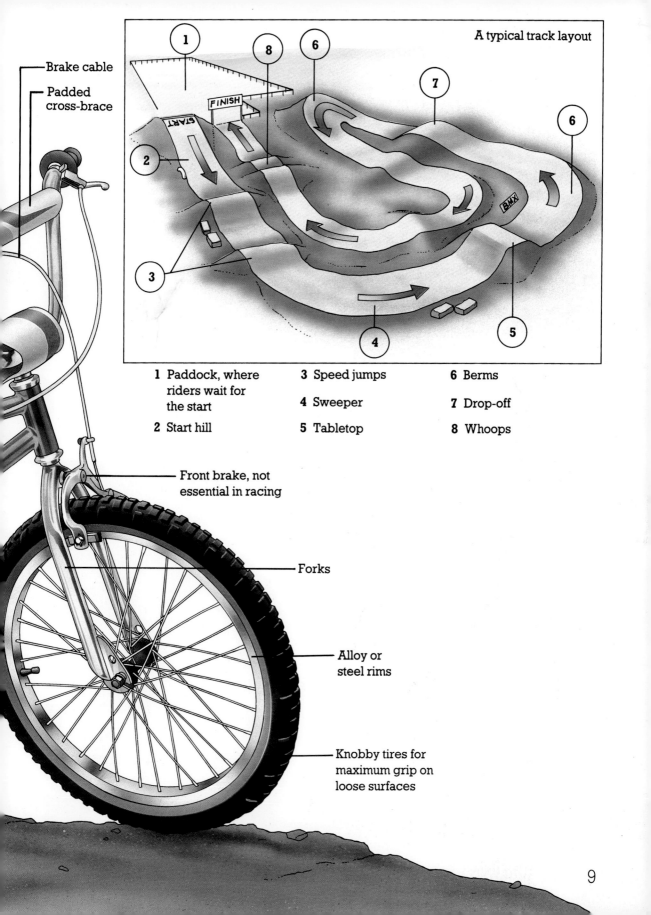

Brake cable

Padded
cross-brace

A typical track layout

FINISH

START

BMX

1 Paddock, where
   riders wait for
   the start
2 Start hill

3 Speed jumps

4 Sweeper

5 Tabletop

6 Berms

7 Drop-off

8 Whoops

Front brake, not
essential in racing

Forks

Alloy or
steel rims

Knobby tires for
maximum grip on
loose surfaces

9

Equipment

BMX competitors wear special safety equipment. It is bright and stylish and gives the rider confidence. Apparatus such as ramps and quarterpipes are used for freestyle practice and displays.

To enjoy BMX riding, however, you do not need to buy expensive gear. The minimum requirements are a helmet, gloves, a long-sleeved top, long pants and running shoes.

▷ The well-dressed and well-protected BMXer wears a special lightweight helmet and has padded pants, elbow guards and gloves. Sturdy shoes to provide a good grip complete the outfit.

▽ A piece of apparatus used for freestyle display is a quarter-pipe. It is a curved ramp that gives the rider extra height.

BMX riding

The basic skills of riding should be mastered before trying special techniques. Learning to control your bike is important. Good practices include stopping with the front wheel dead on a line and riding around a bend while keeping the same distance from the curb.

Simple techniques or tricks include making a slide stop and doing wheelies.

▷ With practice, you can do all kinds of wheelies, riding for some distance on the back wheel and turning or pivoting on it.

▽ The slide stop is best done on loose gravel. The bike is turned sideways toward the direction of travel.

BMX racing

BMX tracks are no more than a few hundred yards long. But they contain enough twists, turns and jumps to test all the riding skills.

Riders start at the top of a hill or ramp and ride down it in lanes. Then there are all kinds of jumps, bumps and turns to negotiate before the finishing straight, in about half a minute of all-out effort.

△ At the start, riders must have their front wheels against the starting board, or gate, and firmly on the ground. A good start is important. Riders aim for the holeshot, the leading position on the first turn.

▷ Farther along the course, the leaders have begun to draw away from the rest.

▷ BMXers use one leg for balance as they take a sharp, flat turn, called a sweeper. Banked turns, called berms, can be taken at top speed and are good places for passing other riders.

Tactics and technique play an important part in racing. Riders race close together, but physical contact is not allowed. You can block a rider behind you, but you may not force a rider off his or her position.

BMX races have events for riders of all ages, from 6 to over-16s. The bigger meetings have thousands of entrants.

Riders in each age group are divided into sets of eight. They take part in three races, or motos, against each other, with different starting positions each time. The most successful riders advance to the next round.

▽ At least one rider gets his jump wrong, and the result is a spectacular crash, or wipeout. When falling, it is advisable to abandon your bike. It is safer to roll on the ground by yourself than to take your bike with you.

In the moto system, one point is awarded for finishing first, two for second and so on. The four riders with the fewest points after their three motos qualify for the next round. In small events, this might be the main, or final.

In the transfer system, the winners of the first and second motos qualify without racing again, and the first and second in the third moto also advance.

△ The joy of winning. Trophies and prizes are awarded to the winning riders and teams. The top professionals can earn prize money of several thousand dollars in the big championship events.

Freestyling

Freestyle routines are made up of basic tricks or movements.

The wheelie involves balancing or riding on your back wheel. The endo, a head-over-handlebars crash in racing, means balancing on the front wheel in freestyle. Bunny hops are jumps made without the aid of a ramp. Ramps and quarter-pipes are used for many routines.

△ In some routines the freestyler performs gymnastic balances on his bike. This one is called a bar press.

▷ The basic trick of riding up and down a steep ramp or a quarter-pipe gives a freestyler room for spectacular turns at the top. This is a front-wheel kickturn.

◁ A single spectator looks on in admiration as a pair of freestylers shoot skywards. They are both doing a 90° cross-up – turning the handlebars through a right-angle while the front wheel is in the air.

Jumping off a steep ramp in this way, freestylers might have a landing drop of 3 meters (10 ft) or more. Strong bikes are needed for this sort of rough treatment.

Freestyle stars give displays and demonstrations. There are also freestyle competitions. These are judged by a panel of experts, as in ice skating or gymnastics.

In competitions, there are compulsory movements and tricks as well as the competitors' own routines. Judges look for control, imagination and originality.

△ A freestyler demonstrates a crossed-up aerial. Spreading his knees wide, he has crossed over his hands to turn the handlebars around and will turn them back again before landing.

▷ There is no limit to the tricks and balances that can be performed, using hands and legs on all parts of the bike.

△ This is quite a bunny hop! But the brave volunteers on the ground are not worried because it's a champion who is making the jump.

◁ This is called a bar hop. It is done by swinging the legs up under the arms, while the bike is moving forward and sitting on the cross-brace of the handlebars.

Cruisers

Cruisers are larger-scale versions of BMX bikes. They have 61 or 66 cm (24 or 26 in) wheels, compared with 51 cm (20 in) for regular BMX bikes. There are race classes in the higher age groups for cruisers.

△ Cruisers have bigger wheels than regular BMX bikes.

The story of BMX bikes

A new sport

The story of BMX is a short one. BMX racing is a new sport, which started in the United States in the early 1970s. The BMX stands for Bicycle Moto-Cross (X), moto-cross being the cross-country motorcycle sport.

△ A moto in the world championships.

Birth of the BMX bike

Cycling had its own cross-country sport in cyclo-cross. Confined mainly to Europe, cyclo-cross is a stamina-sapping race over several laps of a big course. But cyclo-cross bikes are more like racing machines. When the going gets rough, their riders pick them up and run with them! What was needed was a tough bike that youngsters could use, a bike that could negotiate twists, turns and bumps without

breaking up.

It was in Santa Monica, California, that the first BMX bike was made. In 1969, a bicycle company called Schwinn produced a Stingray bike styled on the moto-cross machines. Youngsters tearing around a moto-cross course on Stingrays were seen in a movie about motorcycling and very soon everyone wanted one of these bikes.

△ Freestyle developed in the late 1970s.

Spread of the sport

The first official BMX race was staged in California in 1971, although it was not until 1973 that the first true BMX bike was built. The sport spread rapidly throughout the United States, and then across the Pacific to Australia and Japan. Holland was the first European country to take up BMX. It reached Britain in 1980 and has since spread to most other parts of the world.

The International BMX Federation was formed in 1981, and organized its first world championships in 1982, at Daytona, Florida.

△ A sidehack, like a sidecar in motorcycling.

BMX expands

While BMX was spreading round the world, the bikes themselves were continually being improved. Riders developed

tricks in practice and in the late 1970s this led to freestyle, a new branch of the sport. Bikes have now been modified especially for freestyle use.

Larger BMX bikes called cruisers were built and this is a version of the sport that is growing in popularity. Sidehacks, the sidecar version, did not catch on, however.

Girls also began to take part in both racing and freestyle. There are special races for girls, but they can also compete against boys.

△ Girls take part in all BMX sport.

Facts and records

Bunny hops

Jumping high obstacles without the aid of a ramp calls for skill and athletic ability. Dave Sanderson set a record height of 107 cm (42 inches) in 1983.

Pedal cross

The sport of BMX racing might have been called pedal cross. That was the name it was first given back in 1969 at Palms Park, Santa Monica, when youngsters first began to race their bikes on dirt trails, copying their moto-cross idols.

Sponsorship

There is plenty of help available for good BMX riders. A local shop might offer a discount on equipment in return for publicity or opinions on new designs. The stars of the sport enjoy full factory sponsorship. As professional sportsmen, they ride as members of a manufacturer's team.

▽ Dave Sanderson, a British champion, demonstrates the technique that earned him the world bunny hop record.

Glossary

Aerial
A mid-air stunt performed from a ramp.

Bar hop
Freestyle trick in which the rider puts his legs through his hands and over the handlebars.

Berm
A banked turn.

Bunny hop
A jump from the flat made without a launching ramp.

Cruiser
A larger BMX bike, often referred to as an all-terrain bicycle.

Drop-off
A track obstacle in which the landing area is at a lower level.

Endo
A forward somersault or a front-wheel balance.

Freestyle
Branch of BMX in which skills and tricks are displayed.

Kickturn
Turning the bike round at the top of a ramp.

Main
The final race of a competition.

Moto
A qualifying race, or heat.

Quarterpipe
A specially curved ramp.

Ramp
A piece of apparatus used for gaining height, or any inclined surface.

Sidehack
A BMX bike fitted with a sidecar.

Speed jump
A small track obstacle that can be taken at fast speeds, or the technique for jumping it.

Sweeper
A flat bend without banking.

Tabletop
A track obstacle with a flat top.

Wheelie
Riding or balancing with the front wheel off the ground.

Whoops
A series of small, closely spaced track jumps.

Index